Boats
Byron Barton

HarperCollins*Publishers*

Copyright © 1986 by Byron Barton. Printed in Hong Kong. All rights reserved.
Library of Congress Cataloging-in-Publication Data   Barton, Byron. Boats. Summary: Depicts
several kinds of boats and ships.   1. Boats and boating—Juvenile literature.   2. Ships—Juvenile
literature.   [1. Boats and boating.   2. Ships.]   I. Title.   VM150.B36   1986   387.2   [E]   85-47900
ISBN 0-694-00059-0.—0-690-04536-0 (lib. bdg.)

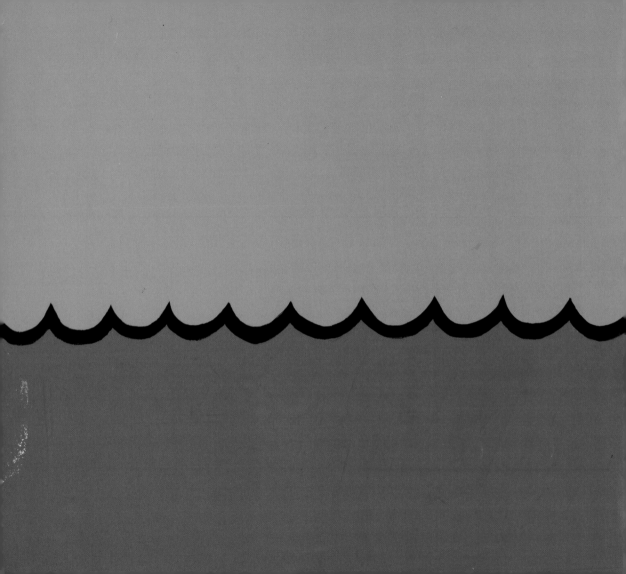

On the water

there goes a rowboat.

Here comes a sailboat

sailing by.

There is a motorboat

speeding through waves.

A fireboat rushes

to put out a fire.

A ferryboat carries

people and cars.

There goes a fishing boat

out to sea.

Here comes a cruise ship

into the harbor.

Here comes a tugboat

to help the ship dock.

Here is the tugboat

pushing and pulling.

Here is the ship

at the dock.

Here are the workers

loading the ship.

Here are the people

going on board.

Here are the people

waving good-bye.

There goes the ship

sailing away.

Bon voyage.